HOTEL UZ

BEKISTAN

ΚΝΩΣΙΩΝ
Ρ

PREFACE

Special Support
Saïda Mirziyoyeva
Head of the Communications and Information Policy Section of the Administration of the President of the Republic of Uzbekistan

We are honoured to present *Unbuild Together. Archaism vs Modernity*, Uzbekistan's third contribution to the Venice Biennale and our second participation in the Architecture Biennale. The theme of this year, *The Laboratory of the Future*, has given us a wonderful opportunity to delve into our rich architectural heritage and explore its potential in shaping the future.

The pavilion is centred around the ancient fortresses called *qalas*, a heritage of the Khorezm civilization. Found throughout the country, they are an enduring symbol of the ingenuity and resilience of the Uzbek people and a testament to the country's long and varied history.

The title of the pavilion *Unbuild Together. Archaism vs Modernity* implies a collaborative effort in understanding the past and how it can inform our present and future. By promoting the significance of *qalas*, we hope to raise awareness of the importance of cultural heritage preservation for the future generations.

Our continued participation in the Venice Biennale helps us to further advance our mission of promoting the culture of Uzbekistan and fostering international cooperation and dialogue. Building up on our previous contributions, we hope that this year's edition will help establish Uzbekistan as a notable and enduring presence at the Venice Biennale. Creating a platform for experiments and a vibrant exchange of ideas, the national pavilion of Uzbekistan increases the visibility of the Uzbek people, their culture, and of the broader Central Asian region.

COMMISSIONER'S PERSPECTIVE

Gayane Umerova
Executive Director of the Art and Culture Development Foundation of the Republic of Uzbekistan

Learning from traditional materials, forms, and techniques offers an opportunity to recover forgotten knowledge and bring back ideas and approaches that can help address some of the pressing problems we are facing today.

A key element of Uzbekistan's architectural heritage, traditional Uzbek bricks play a central role in our national pavilion this year. Bricks are both a universal and archaic material, and they have been used in building construction in Uzbekistan for centuries. They are known for their durability and can last for centuries, making them a great choice for long-lasting building projects.

The theme announced by curator Leslie Lokko, *The Laboratory of the Future*, envisions the Biennale as a kind of workshop, a laboratory where participants and the audience imagine what the future can hold. In response to this theme, we decided to look into our past to seek a vision for our shared future. This year, we address different horizons of Uzbekistan's architectural heritage as a potential tool to envision the future and a key element to challenge the dominant concept of modernity.

Called *Unbuild Together. Archaism vs Modernity*, the pavilion is a major collaborative effort. It brings together a diverse group of curators, researchers, craftsmen, and artists to explore the ruins of the *qalas*, the ancient fortresses of the Karakalpakstan and the heritage of the Khorezmian civilization. French-Moroccan architecture office Studio KO brings a wealth of international experience and expertise in architectural design, while the students and professors of Ajou University in Tashkent bring a deep understanding of Uzbekistan's architectural tradition. Artists Abdulvahid Bukhoriy, El Mehdi Azzam, Miza Mucciarelli, and Emine Gözde Sevim add their unique perspectives expanding the dimensions of this research-based project.

To deepen our understanding of these ancient fortresses we have also collaborated with one of the leading experts on the archaeology of qalas, Dr Irina Arzhantseva, who wrote a book on Sergey Tolstov's expeditions exploring the ruins of *qalas* in the twentieth century. The groundbreaking work of Tolstov was one of the first scientific studies of *qalas* and their place in Uzbekistan's rich history. He documented the architecture and engineering of the *qalas* in great detail and also collected artefacts from the surrounding areas. The scope and depth of Dr Arzhantseva's knowledge help us to approach the *qalas* and the traditional techniques used in their construction with scientific accuracy. Her research also provides valuable insight into the relationship between the *qalas* and the surrounding communities, and how these structures have shaped the region's identity over time.

Looking to the future, our ancient heritage can help us rethink the current trajectory of global development and the role architecture plays in shaping our collective destiny. By examining the architectural remains of past societies, we can gain insight into the values, beliefs, and technologies that shaped their worlds. This in turn can inform our own design choices and decision-making as we work to build a better and more sustainable future.

CURATOR'S STATEMENT

Studio KO, Karl Fournier & Olivier Marty
Architects, founders of Studio KO

This installation is an invitation to sit at the table of history. To step aside and to take time to pause from the ever-accelerating progression of the world.

In order to illustrate this Biennale's theme of *The Laboratory of the Future*, we wished to welcome the human being at the heart of all architectural practice.

With this in mind, we gave twenty-five architecture students from the Ajou University in Tashkent the opportunity to participate in a collaborative workshop, a journey through their own history, from the Qalas of Karakapalstan to the glazed domes of Bukhara through the modernism of the Soviet era.

It became a story of encounter and transmission in which we were no more than couriers, awakening the consciousness of the students who already carried deep within themselves the knowledge of who they are and from where they speak.

In the way it is carried out and constructed, the project could be inscribed in a pre-Enlightenment Universalism, that of the great merchant voyages between Venice and Central Asia, on that long path linking the West and the East.

This journey together through time and space was an opportunity to address many themes that are close to our hearts and that we consider universal enough to share with everyone. It was therefore as much a question of context as of materiality.

Accompanying us on this journey were architects Jean-Baptiste Carisé and Sophia Bengebara from our studio along with several artists whose practice reflexively questions the world: film director El Mehdi Azzam, visual artist Miza Mucciarelli, and photographer Emine Gözde Sevim.

Together, from different backgrounds, we experienced immersion, shared discoveries, questions, and discussions; we broached parts of history until we could ask ourselves to begin conceiving architecture.

Thus, while walking through the ruins and listening to the historian and archaeologist Irina Arzhantseva's erudite presentation of the Tolstov expedition, many of the students, when asked to explore a scenography for their national pavilion at the Venice Architecture Biennale, arrived at the form of the labyrinth, confirming our initial intuition.

It is a structure reduced to its most abstract expression, with a potent evocative force and an allegorical capacity to describe our time.

Then it was a question of thinking about building, and everyone was offered a game of brick assembly and modular composition. The result was an abundance of blocks, reliefs, stairs, shadows, and patterns. This was the time of the material, of Uzbek bricks and the skilful mixtures enamelling their contours under the patient eye of the master ceramist from Bukhara, Abdulvahid Bukhoriy.

Meanwhile, in Tashkent, in the artic cold and with little fanfare, a 1:1 scale prototype of the project was built, a labyrinthine structure of wooden formwork planks, a palisade unravelled into space.

In an unsettling analogy, we chose to house it in the Imperial-era Diesel Station, the future Centre for Contemporary Arts, because of its striking resemblance to the pavilion of the Arsenale in Venice, separated by several centuries and thousands of kilometres.

This back and forth from observation to thought and from thought to hand, this trial and error, this experimentation with things, is precious and fundamental, because it initiates the making of a project; it allows for the unexpected to emerge. These are the tools of the architect. But, in the end, after the critical sieve of the eye and the conscience, what is left?

An architectural installation that confronts commonly accepted temporal boundaries, builds unexpected bridges between eras, and attempts to deconstruct, to unbuild, the opposition between archaism and modernity. A form that proves nothing about architecture.

A structure of which one does not know whether it is ephemeral or pre-existing; whether it is made of brick remains from Venetian construction sites that sometimes open up, leaving a passageway, an interstice where a piece of copper oxide from Central Asia is nestled.

It is an opaque path that projects at its core a film that is the embodiment and impressions of our moments of sharing and creation.

At the exit, two moments are highlighted as an echo of the experience. First, a model that offers the necessary vantage point for understanding; a view above the labyrinth. And second, a light table that reveals traces, fragments, drawings, student research, failed attempts, and anomalies; we call them relics.

And if the magic works, sometimes all that remains is a memory, the impression of opacity, the fleeting disturbance of feeling lost; the comfort of a fortress, the surprise of a shard of radiant turquoise in the dark.

THE RUINS OF KHOREZM:
An Archive of Lost Architecture

Irina Arzhantseva
Principal Researcher in the Institute of Ethnology and Anthropology, Russian Academy of Sciences

Khorezm, an ancient historical region in Central Asia, is located in an oasis on the lower Amu Darya river (Oksa) in modern Uzbekistan (Autonomous Karakalpakstan) and Turkmenistan. In ancient times, a unique civilisation grew up and flourished there, whose wealth and diversity were based on complex irrigation systems, as well as Khorezm's key position on caravan trade routes and on the borders between nomadic and settled populations. To this day, the lands occupied by the ancient Khorezmian irrigation system are a unique phenomenon, where archaeological monuments and the remains of ancient irrigation systems and planning have been perfectly preserved in the desert. Many prominent orientalists have been interested in Khorezm — Vasily Bartold, for instance, who understood very well what the archaeological and ethnographic material from Khorezm might mean for the history of Central Asia, and emphasised that the study of Khorezm was of great interest, particularly in relation to ethnography, because "... in Khorezm, which is surrounded by desert, like England, which is surrounded by sea, the whole of life took on a unique form, and even features borrowed from outside took on a vitality all of their own."[1]

This region has long attracted travellers and scholars due to its wealth of monumental ruins, strange labyrinths, towers and walls that captured the imagination of anyone seeing them for the first time, with their network of artificial irrigation canals covered in sand, and scattered fragments of pottery covering the *takyrs* around the ruins with a brilliant red carpet. It was a unique conservation area and archaeological "Klondike". Archaeologists had already arrived there by the late 1920s (the expeditions of Aleksandr Yakubovsky in 1928–29, M. Voevodsky in 1934 and the Tashkent archaeologist Yahyo Gulyamov in 1936). However, in order to research this world, which had been completely submerged beneath the sands, a large, multi-disciplinary expedition was needed with great scientific, technical, administrative and financial potential. The Khorezmian Archaeological and Ethnographic Expedition led by the talented and energetic scholar Sergei Tolstov was such an expedition. To quote his vivid expression, "we had to read the great book of Khorezm."

The Khorezmian Archaeological and Ethnographic Expedition of the Institute of Ethnography of the Academy of Sciences of the Soviet Union (1937–1997) was the largest and longest lasting expedition not only in the Soviet Union but in world archaeology. In terms of the territory covered, the number of monuments studied, the quantity of published material and the organisational complexity and multifaceted approach to the archaeological and ethnographic research, this expedition still has no equal. The Khorezmian Expedition is perhaps the only one to which such a large quantity of popular scientific and artistic literature has been devoted. The work undertaken by the Khorezmian Expedition was carried out on the territory of three republics, Uzbekistan, Kazakhstan and Turkmenistan, covering an area of several hundred thousand square kilometres. However, the main area of interest, the "centre stage" and place where the most extensive research took place during the entire duration of the work, was Khorezm itself.

One cannot overestimate the part played by the Khorezmian expedition and Sergei Tolstov in the shaping of contemporary historical studies in Uzbekistan and Turkmenistan, and the creation of archaeological, ethnographic and historic architectural schools in Central Asia. The well-known Uzbek scholar and academician, Yahyo Gulyamov, Tolstov's colleague and friend, assessed the enormous contribution of the Khorezmian expedition and its leader as follows:

> When it comes to studying Uzbekistan's ancient past, and that of Central Asia in general, it is impossible not to mention the historian, archaeologist, ethnographer, Corresponding Member of the Academy of Sciences of the Soviet Union and Doctor of Historical Sciences, Professor Sergei Tolstov. It is indeed thanks to his tireless activities and the zeal with which he uncovered the ancient secrets of the distant past and his enormous contribution to the study of Central Asian history, that he became famous not only in the Soviet Union, but he also achieved world-wide recognition as an extraordinary scholar. [...] Of all the expeditions I've known, there has never been such a disciplined, energetic and versatile one as the Khorezmian expedition. It was like a research institute [...]

Tolstov's obsession with, and love for, Central Asia and Khorezm can be explained not only by his scholarly interests, although it was, in fact, this very interest in the enigmatic Khorezm — that "Central Asian Egypt" to use Tolstov's metaphorical expression — which was the reason for the fairly successful field seasons, rich in discoveries, that took place before the war.

During the Second World War, in 1941, "The city of bread," as Tashkent was called, took in and saved thousands of evacuees from the western and central parts of the Soviet Union affected by the war. A large number of staff from academic research institutes, including leading scholars affiliated to the institutes of history, oriental studies and the history of material culture and so forth in Moscow and Leningrad had all gravitated to Tashkent, and having formed "Tashkent groups" there, continued their academic research in close collaboration with scientists from the Academy of Sciences of the Uzbek Soviet Socialist Republic. Having been wounded at the frontline, Tolstov also arrived in Tashkent where he found the majority of his colleagues from academic institutions in Moscow and Leningrad — a large number of orientalists, archaeologists, historians and ethnographers, and besides these he met up once again with Uzbek academics whom he had known for a long time and with whom he had forged academic connections long before the war. Among these, the closest to him was Yahyo Gulyamov who had begun historical and archaeological research at Khorezm even earlier than Tolstov.

In 1942, in Tashkent, Tolstov defended his doctoral thesis which was based on his manuscript concerning his monumental work on material from pre-war research carried out in Khorezm. It was entitled *Ancient Khorezm: A Record of Historical and Archaeological Research*. The well-known historian of science and long-standing participant in the Khorezmian expeditions, M. Rozhanskaya, had this to say about this work and its author:

> The thesis mentioned above was prepared in connection with written accounts and ethnographic data and re-worked as the book *Ancient Khorezm*, which came out in 1948 and received the Stalin Prize (USSR State Prize) in 1949. The scale of the work in terms of both, breadth and variety of source material in different languages is truly astounding, and this impressed those who came across it in the course of their scientific and organisational duties. Sergei had quite literally fantastic linguistic abilities which contributed greatly to the research [...][2]

Although only material uncovered during the pre-war field season (1937–40) was used in the book, this work is even now without equal among the many works on the history and archaeology of Khorezm. An extraordinary number of discoveries were made during the pre-war years: medieval castles that once flourished in the Berkut-Qala and Kavat-Qala oases, the ancient fortresses of the magnificent Ayaz-Qala, the majestic palace city of Toprak-Qala and the mysterious and beautiful Koi-Krylgan-Qala which resembled an enchanted labyrinth.

During this time and afterwards, an unusually large number of field plans were made and measurements taken by the expedition due to the fact that, from 1938 onwards, a number of professional architects and graduates and students from the All Union Academy of Architecture worked on the expedition, including I. N. Tikhomirova (1938), V. I. Pilyavsky and G. Ali-Zadeh (1939) and V. A. Lavrov, M. A. Orlov and V. I. Pentman (1940). Tolstov's brother Nikolai, an artist by training, also took part in the expedition during these years and afterwards, and in

1950 the artist I. V. Savitsky joined the expedition. The latter went on to found the famous museum in Nukus, "The Louvre of the Desert."

During the post-war years, the work carried out by the Khorezmian Expedition evolved along new methodological lines and grew considerably in scale. This was truly the "golden age" of the expedition. The Khorezmian Expedition became one of the greatest and most technically advanced archaeological expeditions in the Soviet Union. As M. A. Itina, one of Tolstov's students and associates, put it:

> [...] He obtained support for his expedition in those difficult times both from central government and from the local authorities of the Karakalpak Republic. Several parties were working in different regions of Central Asia at the same time. They had planes, portable generators and whole caravans of special vehicles at their disposal.[3]

Routes for those on foot or in vehicles or planes covered the whole desert area containing the ancient irrigation systems in the lower reaches of the Amu Darya River — Ancient Khorezm. The expedition was reorganised after 1945 so that it comprised both archaeology and ethnography. Its composition meant that the work was not purely ethnographical. In the field the scientific team included representatives from many related professions — geographers, geomorphologists (including the famous scientist Aleksandra Kes), land surveyors and soil analysts worked alongside the archaeologists because particular attention was paid to the study of the ancient irrigation systems, the former courses taken by the Amu Darya and Syr Darya rivers, the problem of the channels through the ancient river bed of the Uzboy, and palaeoclimatic reconstructions. Tolstov's undoubted merit lies in his use of aerial survey methods, unprecedented in their scale for that time, not only for our country but for world archaeology as a whole. For a period of ten successive years starting in 1946, several small PO-2 state aviation biplanes operating from the Nukus airfield worked with the KhAEE (Khorezmian Archaeological-Ethnographic Expedition). Even to this day, the archive of aerial photography (more than 5,000 images) has no equal in world archaeology, and its scientific value is immense because since that time (i.e. from the end of the 1940s), most of the terrain in this region has changed beyond all recognition. The expedition continued its work even after the death of Sergei Tolstov, its founder and tireless director, in 1976. The last archaeological work connected with the KhAEE took place in 1996 and 1997 at the Khumbuz Tepa site in the Khorezmian region of Uzbekistan.

The field documentation of the work carried out by the expedition comprises an extensive archive, running to several tens of thousands of items. The archive is currently housed in the Institute of Anthropology and Ethnography of the Russian Academy of Sciences. In addition to the archaeological, anthropological and numismatic collections, the material collected as a result of many years of work on the expedition includes a great many art objects, examples of sculpture and painting, jewellery and ancient Aramaic, Turkic and Arab inscriptions and so on, and numbers more than 3.5 million items. Archive material includes the field diaries kept by researchers, expedition reports and plans as well as a large amount of illustrative material including sketches, copies of wall paintings and drawings of the finds carried out by artists on the expedition like I. V. Savitsky, N. P. Tolstov, V. I. Pentman and G. M. Baev. Part of this archive, the archive containing the photographs from the expedition, is housed separately, and includes negatives (film and glass plate negatives), positives (slides) and prints, as well as several thousand aerial photographs.

This archive of materials accumulated over sixty years of work on the Khorezmian expedition is still a rich source for the history, archaeology, ethnography and architecture of the enchanting country Khorezm.

* * * * * *

NOTES

[1] *Bartol'd 1963, p. 206.*

[2] *Rožanskaja 2013, pp. 12, 13.*

[3] *Itina 1997, p. 191.*

The following pages are taken from the classic monograph by S. P. Tolstov published in 1948 in 3000 copies under the title Ancient Khorezm: The Experience of Historical and Archaeological Research *(M., publishing house of Moscow State University) and* In the Footsteps of the Ancient Khorezmian Civilization *(M.-L., publishing house of USSR Academy of Sciences).*

Only the cover and a few pages of the first volume were selected (pages 99, 101, 114, 115, 116, 117, 120).

Two criteria dictated the choice of pages: the desire to focus on those related to the research around the Qalas ruins and those showing drawings of extraordinary sensitivity and precision. Beyond the scientific value of this research, it is therefore also a matter of emphasising the artistic approach that accompanied the multidisciplinary Khorezmian expedition, which brought together archaeologists, ethnologists as well as artists and architects.

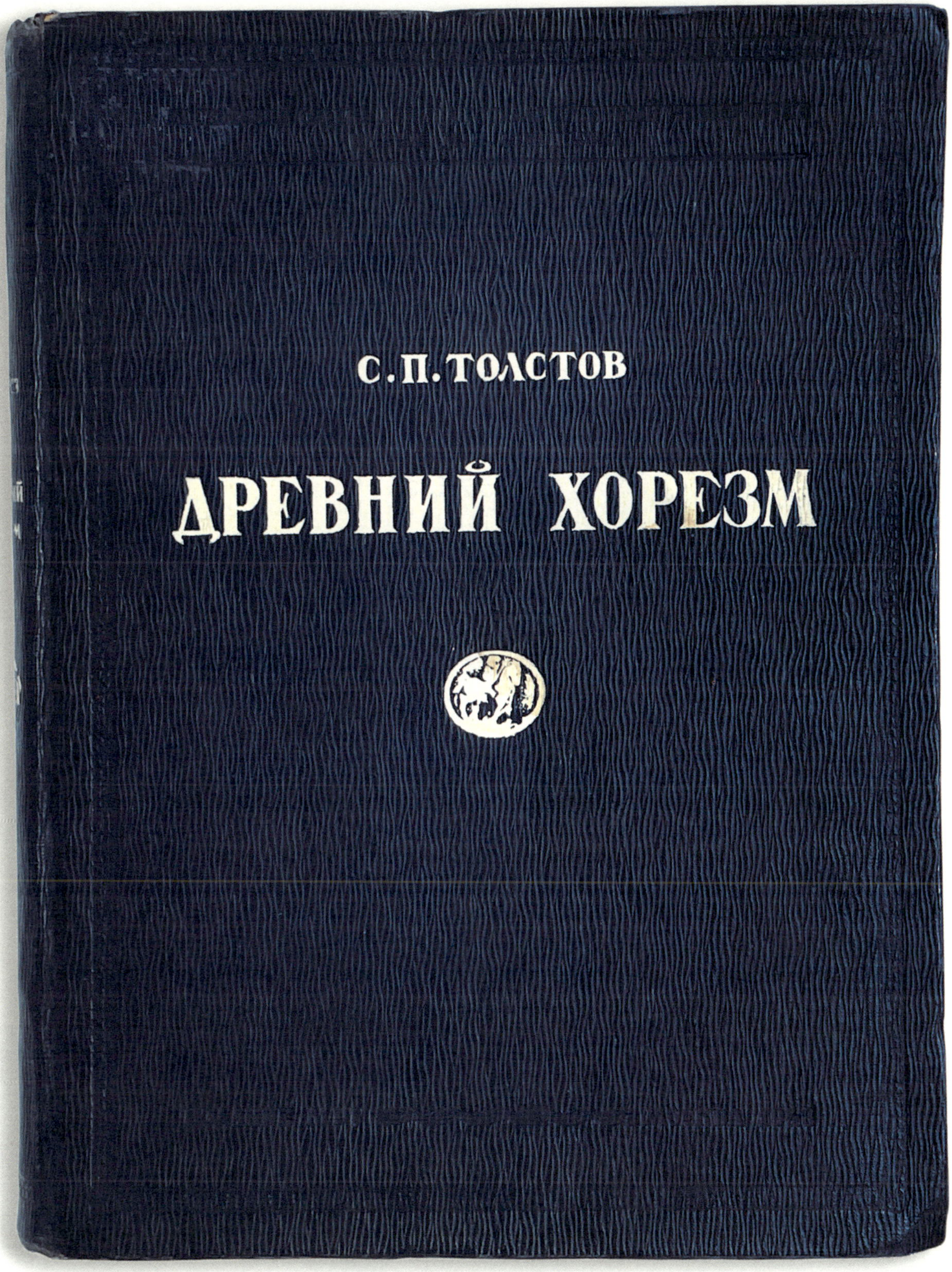
С.П.ТОЛСТОВ
ДРЕВНИЙ ХОРЕЗМ

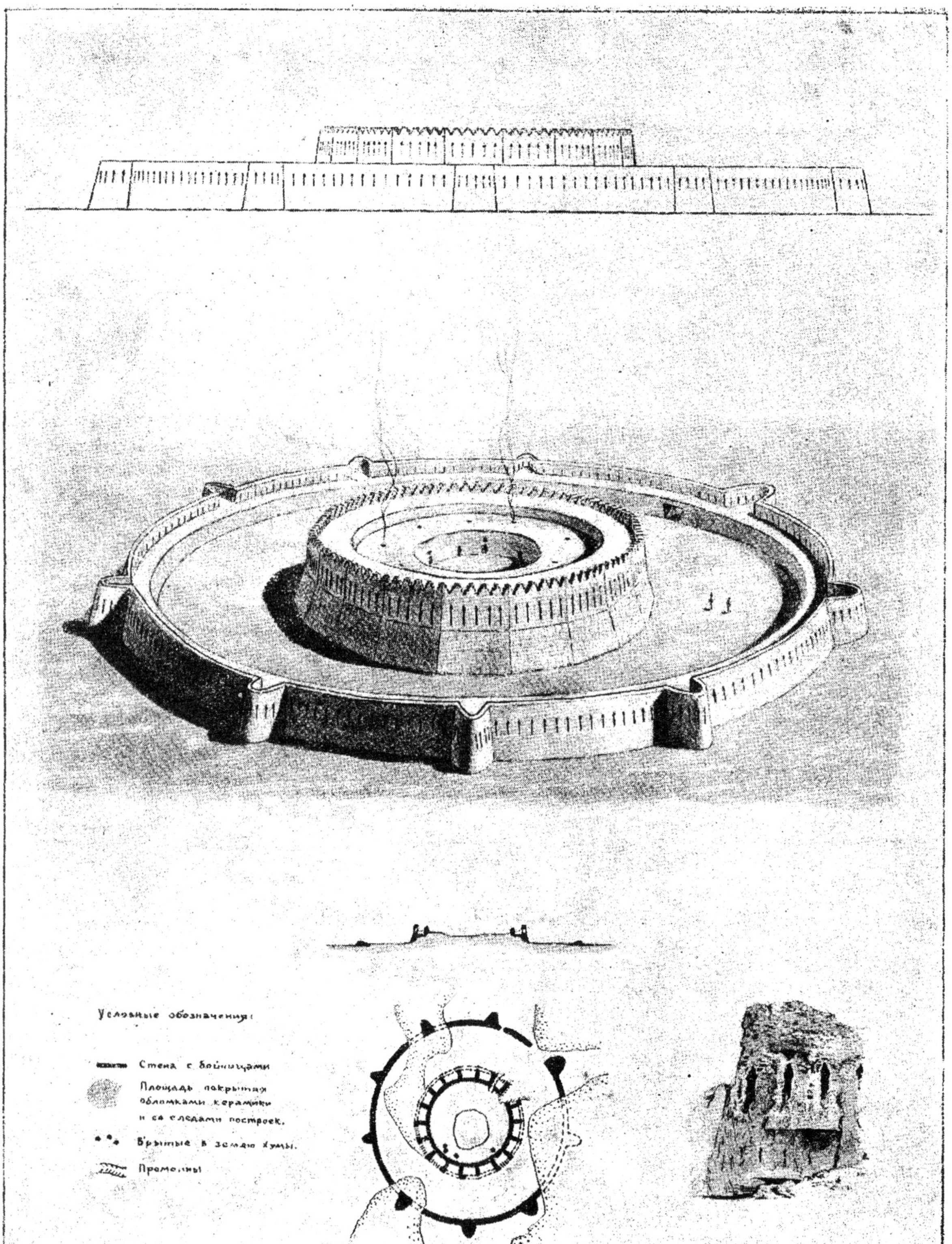

Рис. 34. Кой-крылган-кала. План и разрез (обмеры С. П. Толстова). Реконструкция С. П. и Н. П. Толстовых.

ли-кала (на Чермен-ябе, рис. 36 и 38), Ак-тепе (близ Кават-калы, рис. 37), Кузы-крылган-кала и, наконец, укрепленный дом к югу от Базар-кала.

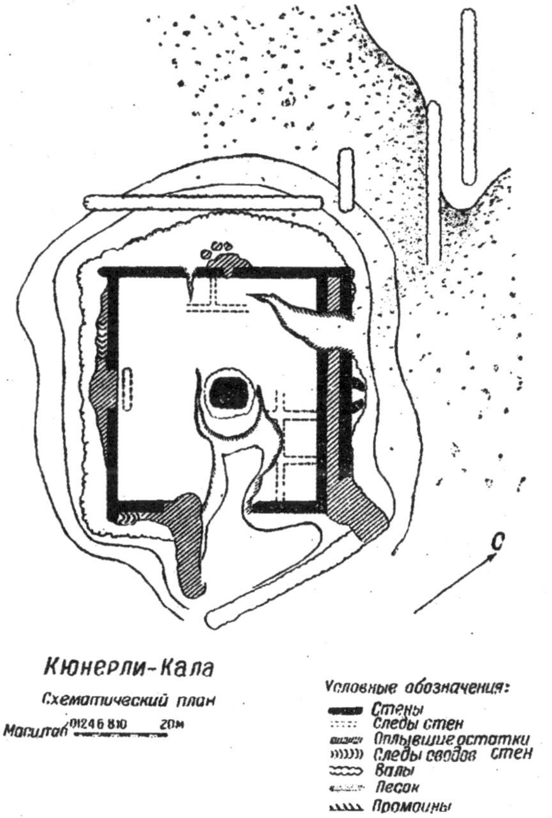

Рис. 36. Кюнерли-кала. План. Обмер С. Толстова и С. Гасанова.

Кюнерли-кала представляет собой мощный, сложенный из сырцового кирпича античных размеров, прямоугольный массив 55 × 55 метров при высоте около 8 метров, не считая поднимающейся еще на 3 метра глиняной башни в центре здания. С ЮВ расположен укрепленный вход, посередине каждой из остальных трех

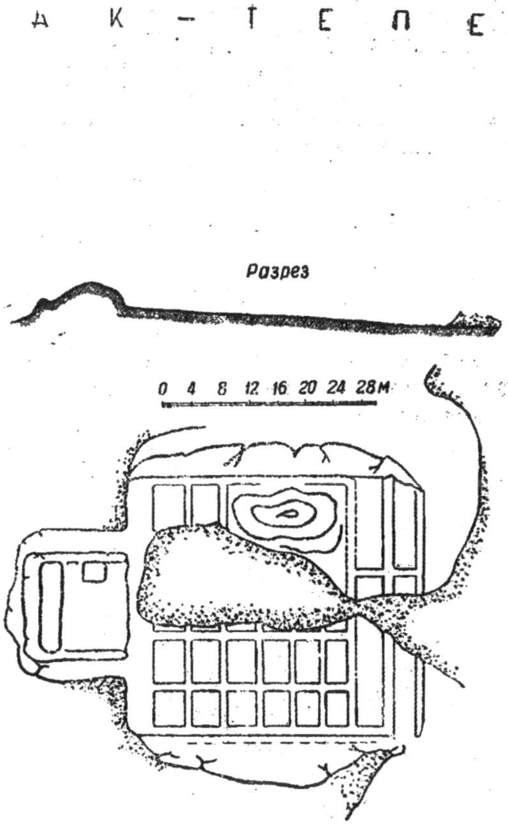

Рис. 37. Ак-тепе. План и разрез. Обмер С. Толстова.

сторон сохранились небольшие башни с бойницами, с СЗ и СВ—следы мощных стен окружающего здание двора. Снаружи здание опо-

Рис. 38. Кюнерли-кала. Общий вид развалин. Рис. Н. Толстова.

ки, принадлежащей к описанному выше кушанскому комплексу, среди которой попадаются терракотовые статуэтки. На развалинах одного дома найдены две медные хорезмийские монеты с изображением царя в орлином шлеме, датируемые нами III в. н. э.[1]

гают толщины 15 см). Кирпичи положены на глиняный раствор, прослойка между кирпичами достигает 8 см.

Ворота, открывающиеся посредине юго-восточной стены крепости, защищены с обеих сторон прямоугольными башнями (5 × 8 м), каж-

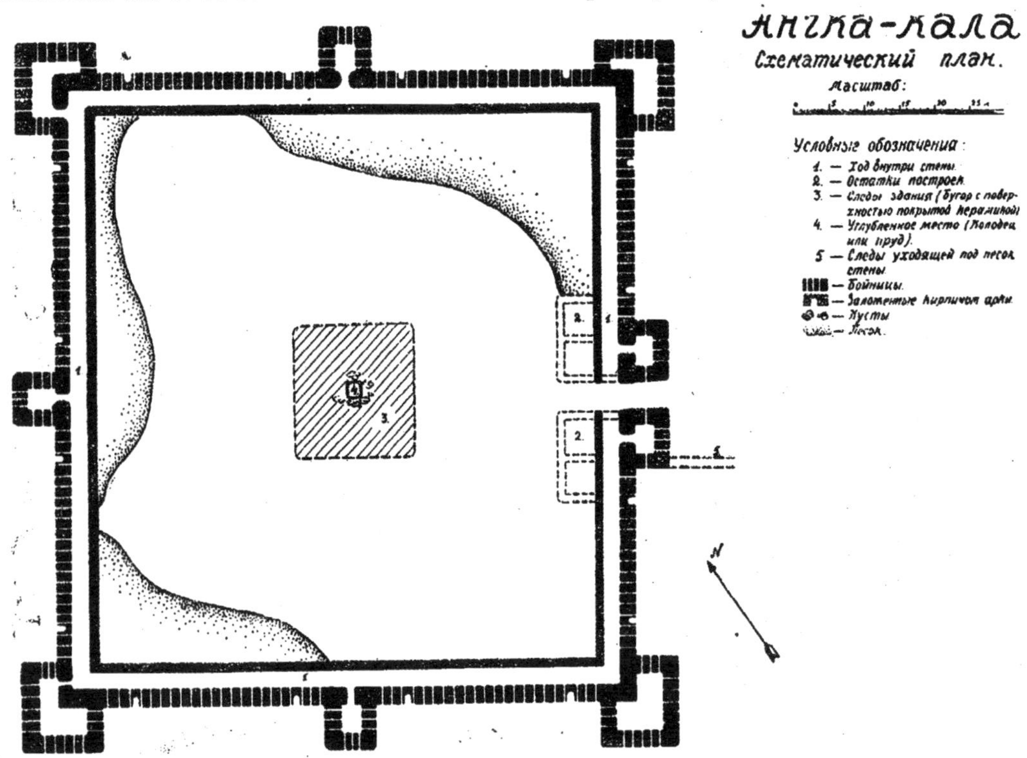

Рис. 50. Ангка-кала. План. Обмер С. П. Толстова.

Ангка-кала отличается от других античных крепостей Хорезма сравнительно небольшими размерами. Она образует правильный квадрат

дая из которых открывается внутрь ворот одной бойницей.

На каждом из углов расположена квадратная

Рис. 51. Калалы-гыр № 2. Перспектива. Рис. худ. Н. П. Толстова.

75 × 75 м, обнесенный типичной для античных крепостей двойной стеной, сложенной из очень крупного квадратного сырцового кирпича размером 40 × 40 × 10 см (иногда кирпичи дости-

башня, средним размером 11 × 11 м. План башни крайне своеобразен, резко отличаясь от угловых сооружений всех других крепостей. Башня как бы облекает с двух сторон входящий в нее угол крепости.

Посредине каждой из остальных трех стен располагается одна прямоугольная башня пло-

[1] См. цитированную нами выше статью в ВДИ, 1938, № 4, а также ниже, гл. IV, 1.

щадью 5×7 м. Башня, как правило, выше, чем стена. Сохранившаяся высота башен превышает сохранившуюся высоту стен на 1—3 м.

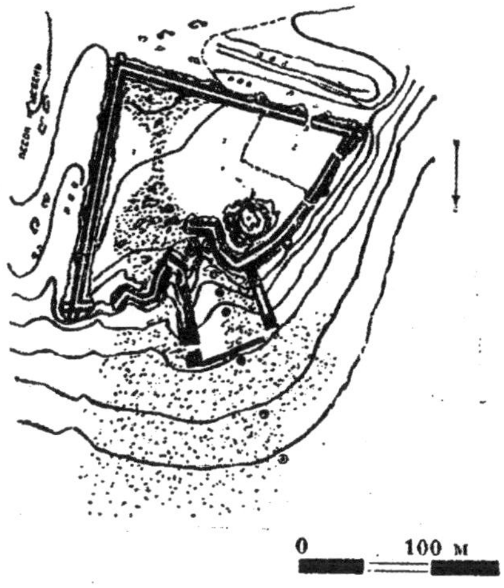

Рис. 52. Калалы-гыр № 2. План. Обмер С. П. Толстова.

Внешняя стена, имеющая посредине высоты толщину около 2 м, открывается наружу рядом обычных для античных крепостей и описанных нами выше высоких и узких бойниц (внешний раствор 1,90 м, внутренний 1,20 м, ширина 25 м, расстояние между бойницами—1,30 м). Низ бойниц расположен на высоте около 4,30 м над уровнем окружающей земли. Стены сохранились на высоту 7 м.

Характерной деталью системы обороны Ангка-калы является наличие по обоим краям каждого простенка между башнями открывающихся наружу круглоарочных дверей 80 см ширины, расположенных на расстоянии около 4 м от башен. Нижний край арок соответствует нижнему краю бойниц. Все арки заложены кирпичом. Повидимому, они были предназначены для вылазок.

Посредине двора крепости расположен плоский, низкий квадратный бугор 18×18 м, с квадратным же, около 2,5×2,5 м, углублением посредине, вокруг которого расположена группа кустарника. Повидимому, это остатки дома с колодцем или прудом посредине. Керамика, грудами лежащая посредине этого бугра, по своему типу примыкает к керамике X—XII вв., характерной для развалин раннемусульманского времени в окрестностях Нариджана, резко отличаясь от керамики, покрывающей окрестные крепости.

Это говорит о том, что крепость, как и некоторые другие, продолжала в какой-то мере использоваться много позднее времени ее постройки и интенсивной жизни в ее окрестностях.

Ряд отмеченных выше отличий от обычного типа античных крепостей, особенно размеры, устройство ворот и тип башен, заставляет видеть в Ангка-кала одно из поздних произведений античной военной архитектуры Хорезма. На это указывают и монетные находки в ее окрестностях, позволяющие датировать ее III—IV в. н. э.

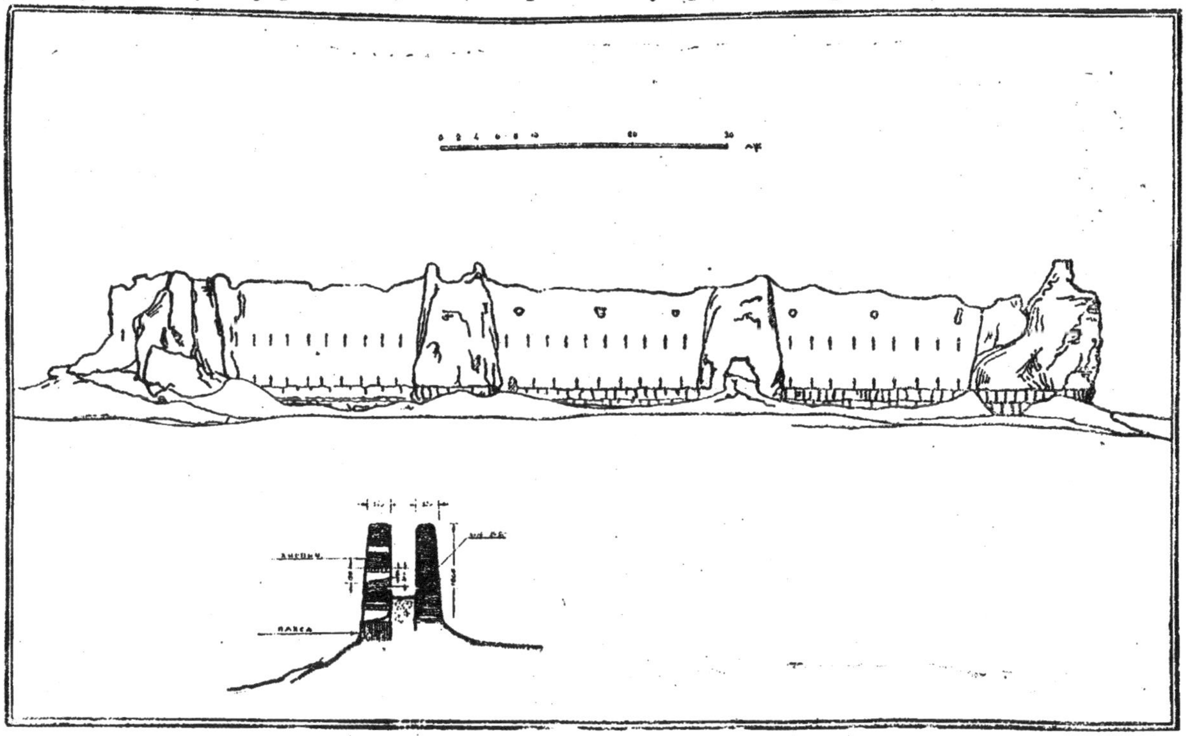

Рис. 53. Гяур-кала (Султан Уиз-даг; фасад). Обмер худ. Н. П. Толстова.

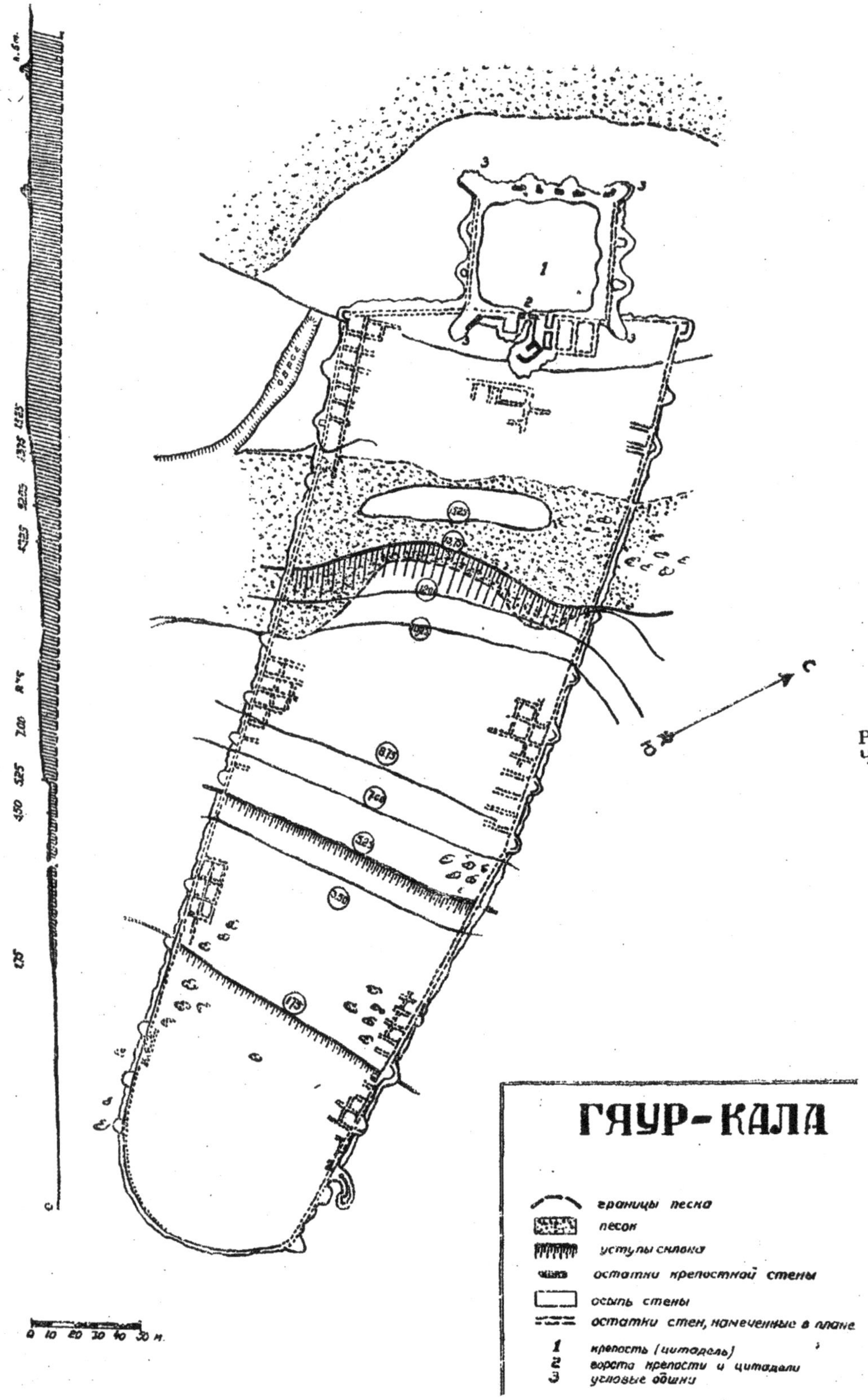

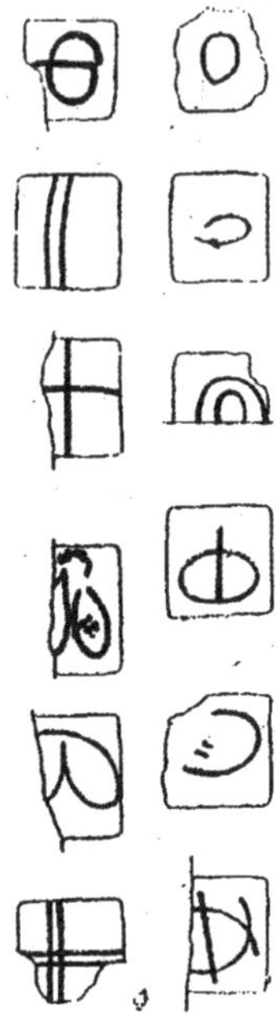

Рис. 55. Гяур-кала на Чермен-ябе. Тамги на кирпичах.

Рис. 54. Гяур-кала на Чермен-ябе (план). Обмер С. П. Толстова и С. С. Гасанова.

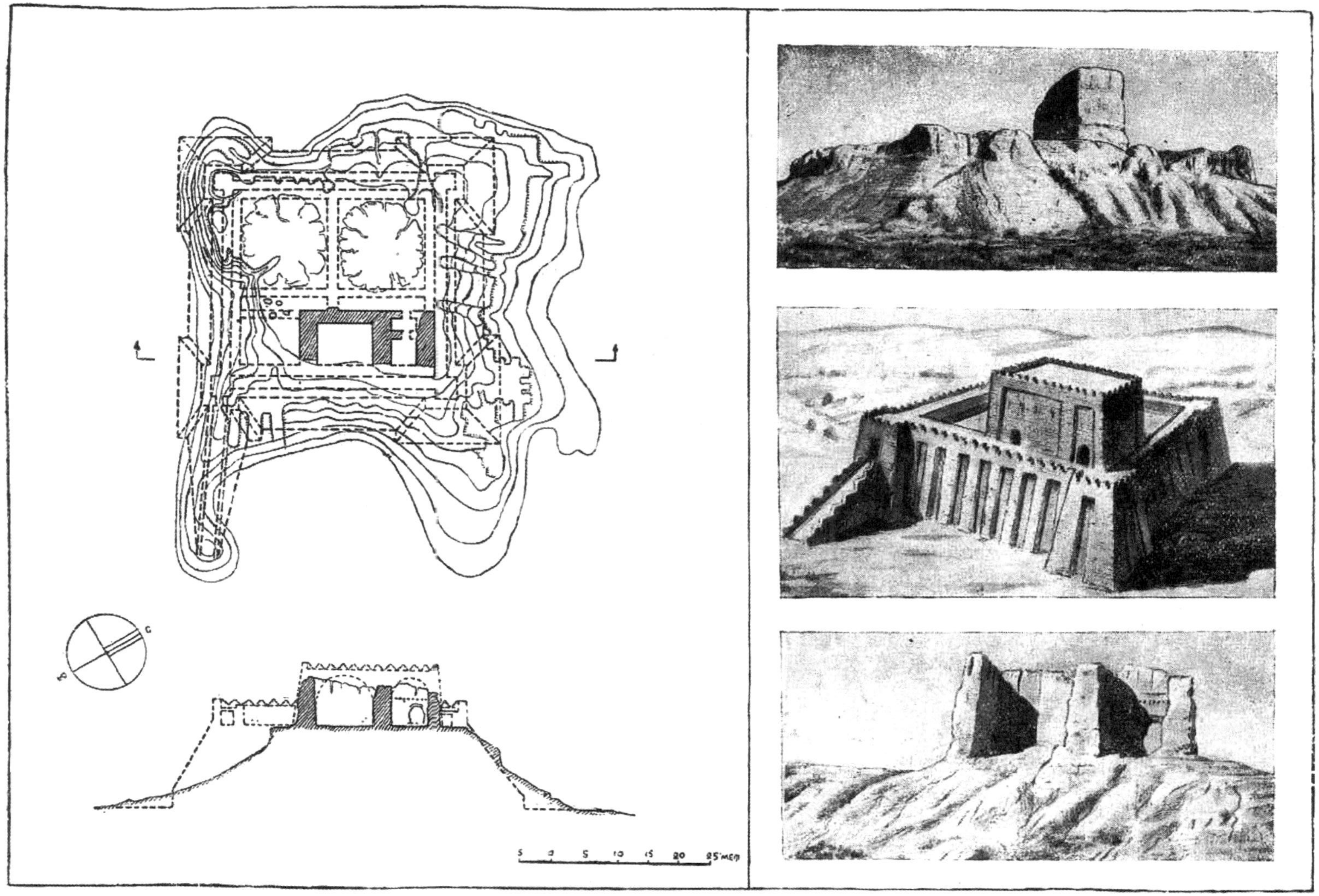

Рис. 56. Джильдык-кала. Обмер арх. В. А. Лаврова.

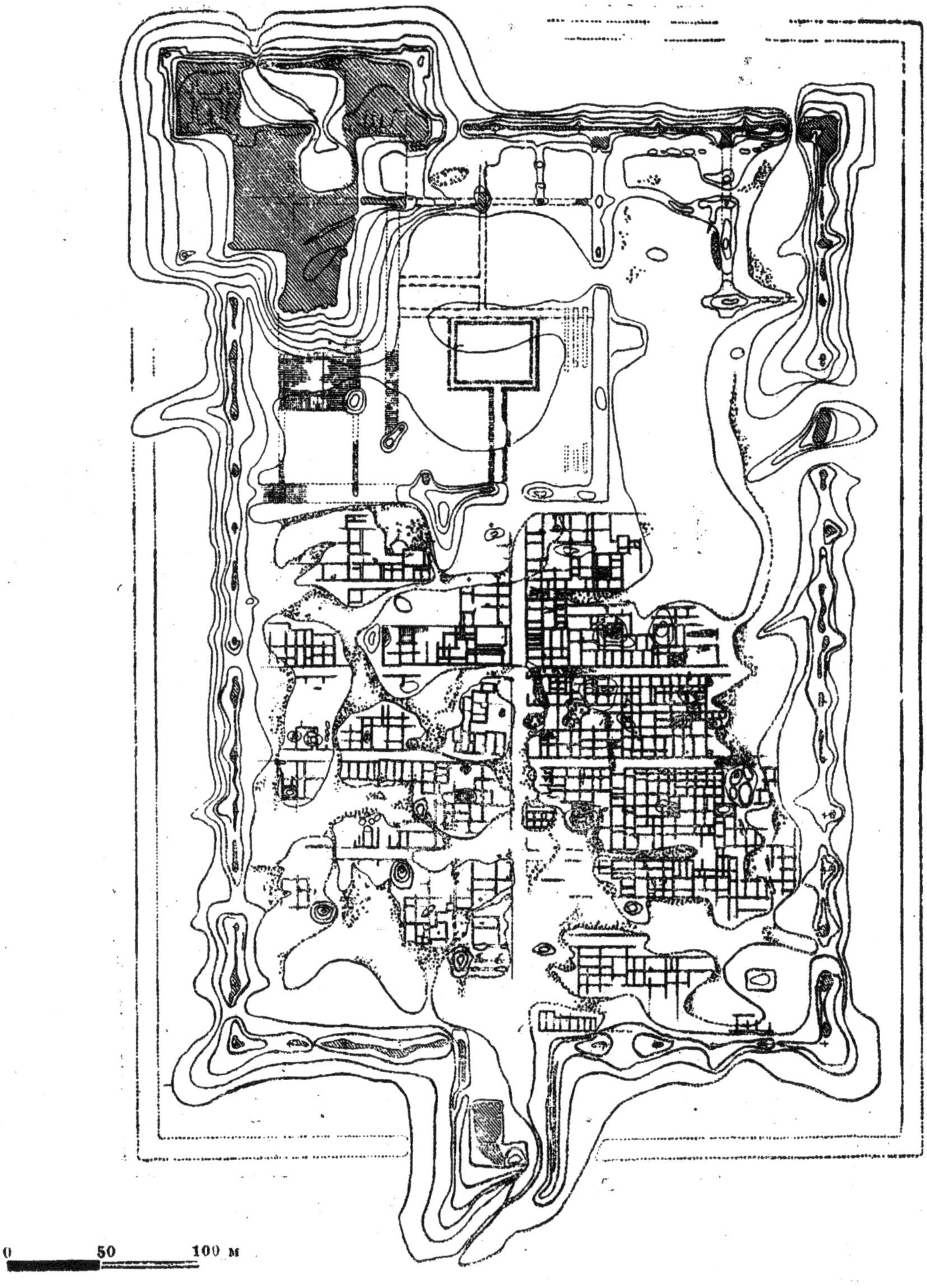

Рис. 62. Топрак-кала. План. Обмеры С. П. Толстова, В. И. Лаврова, М. А. Орлова, В. Пилявского.

IGOR SAVITSKY

Oktyabr Dospanov
Head of the Department of Archaeology at the Karakalpakstan State Museum of Art named after I. V. Savitsky

Today, when mankind is about to leave the first quarter of the twenty-first century behind, the history of the Ancient Khorezmian civilisation is at the forefront of the minds of many of us — a civilisation that has for some time remained a closely guarded secret in the formation of Central Asian culture as a whole. Undoubtedly, Sergei Pavlovich Tolstov (1907–1976), an outstanding twentieth-century scholar, played an important part in uncovering these historical processes right from the start to the acme of his achievement. From whatever angle we view the history of the Khorezmian state, we cannot imagine it without taking into account the Khorezmian archaeological and ethnographic expedition set up by the scholar in the second half of the 1930s.

Sergei Tolstov, who led the expedition for many years, not only uncovered the world of the "Ancient Khorezmian civilisation" but managed to attract an entourage of brilliant young specialists including archaeologists, ethnographers and artists.

Among the enthusiasts invited to take part, we can confidently name the creator of the Nukus Museum of Art, Igor Vitalyevich Savitsky, who devoted his life to putting together a unique collection of art from Ancient Khorezm, decorative art created by people from the Aral Sea region and art by Karakalpak, Uzbek and Russian artists. Because he was a follower of the Khorezm expedition, he managed to set up an archaeological and ethnographic expedition with museum funding, and these continue to this day.

As the author of these lines, I feel very proud that I was one of his followers and an archaeologist while still a student apprentice, and that I received an education and attained a measure of scholastic achievement in this school. Having first met Savitsky in 1979, today I am attempting to pass on my knowledge to the young generation in this museum. This is probably a continuation of the very distinctive links in a chain once initiated by Sergei Tolstov.

The colours of the dry dunes, the rare flowers of Kyzylkum and the ancient and medieval ruins keeping age-old legendary secrets within them attracted Igor Savitsky and drew him like a magnet. It was as if the various artefacts uncovered on the excavations were beckoning him into a conversation with time, reflecting the culture and art of the peoples and tribes who inhabited these regions. I often saw his face, tanned by the desert sun, light up radiantly at the discovery of a beautiful artefact uncovered from an archaeological dig. The colours of the desert and oases, which he depicted with such care, as though creating a temporal link with today, survive in many of his works.

The variety of Igor Savitsky's interests and his appreciation for the decorative arts of the peoples of the Aral Sea region led him to distant villages — *kishlaks*, where they lived and created popular art, preserving the old traditions connected with both nomadic and settled agricultural culture. It was here that he found unique solace for his soul as he admiringly contemplated and studied the whimsical decorations on embroideries and the ornaments and shapes in the various forms of adornment. It goes without saying that he found numerous links between all these and the spiritual world of ancient culture and its religious and philosophical views. It was a revelation to the artist that he was able to refute the view held by a number of scholars who believed that the Steppe peoples had no form of decorative wood carving. His tireless quest culminated in a substantial monograph entitled *Popular Decorative Art of the Karakalpaks: Wood Carving* (1963).

All this laid the foundations for the future museum of art that he created in Nukus.

In addition to collecting and increasing the museum's holdings, he paid great attention to the storage and restoration of the exhibits as they came into the museum. Most of them arrived in very poor condition and in a state in which they were unfit for exhibition. They could be anything from archaeological artefacts to works of popular applied art and paintings. Realising that it was important and necessary, its own school of restoration was gradually established at the museum for ceramics, metalwork, painting and graphic art. Its chief founders include the following: Zh. Kuttymuratova, M. Kalilaeva, A. Shpade, E. Zholdasova and R. Kovalevu, thanks to whom the school is still expanding and continues to preserve the museum's heritage.

I remember Igor Savitsky not only as the director and founder of the museum's collection, but as a very hard worker. The museum was like a home to him, and he could practically be found there round the clock. Of course, as he felt himself at home there, he treated the museum like any good owner would. He was not afraid to clean and wash the floors, and he planted wild flowers in the small museum garden and weeded it; most of all, he loved autumn asters, with which he often decorated the galleries.

Today, the museum contains a large number of artefacts, handed over to it by the Khorezmian Archaeological-Ethnographic Expedition, including archaeological and ethnographic finds which are masterpieces of ancient and medieval culture. They came into the museum thanks to the close links between Igor Savitsky and the scholars of that period. Tatiana Zhdanko, who made far-reaching plans and established directions for the study of the ethnic culture of the people from the Aral Sea region, undoubtedly played a crucial role in this. Thanks to her talent and unwavering commitment, the museum's collection was enlarged through the addition of new decorative and applied art objects, but a distinctive school of ethnographers was founded for which Igor Savitsky must also take credit.

Many of my memories of the relationship between us are not only connected with museum work, but also our shared trips on archaeological expeditions. A particularly touching incident took place in 1982 when our expedition arrived to take part in an excavation of a medieval feudal castle in the Kavat-Qala oasis. However, in place of the monument, we found a huge ditch for the foundations of a new building. We later discovered that the archaeological site had been destroyed to enable the construction of a contemporary building. Shortly after they had found out that we were part of a research expedition, the builders brought us numerous unique and beautiful ancient artefacts. Then, I saw tears rolling down Igor Savitsky's cheeks. They were tears of grief and indignation at man's inability to preserve the unique masterpieces of the ancient Khorezmian civilisation.

His eyes full of hope for the future and an imminent return to the home territory of the museum have stuck in my mind from my last meeting with Igor Savitsky.

* * * * * *

THE BRICK IN THE OASIS OF BUKHARA

Rocco Rante
Researcher-archaeologist in the Islamic Art Department of the Louvre Museum

"We are all born of earth and water" (*Of Nature*, frg. 33). This is how Xenophanes understood human nature in the sixth century BC. This quotation, taken in the most global sense, fits perfectly into a framework of thinking about mankind, and therefore about civilisation, in which the earth becomes the prime, the founding element of civilisation.

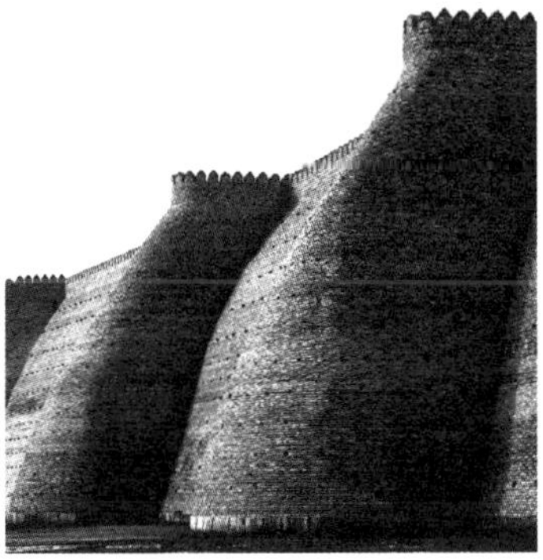

Throughout human history, earth has been used to receive the deceased in prehistoric times, and then to cover them so that the earth, and therefore nature, can take care of them and their souls.
Earth was also used to paint and to paint oneself, and then to make the first tools of daily life: pots, vases, gourds.
The rise of agriculture in the Neolithic period brought about an important change. Man had already mastered the process of drying earth, simply by exposing it to the sun, in order to create structural elements. The mud brick thus made its appearance. The mastery of this new material also required the knowledge of degreasing agents: natural elements such as straw or pebbles, which were mixed with earth and water to obtain a solid and stable final material. The choice of sediment was also crucial. Standardisation of the production process was introduced. Soil was used to create private spaces, barriers, to defend against animals and to protect the cultivated field.
Knowledge of this material has highlighted its structural qualities, but also its fragility, which is linked to its durability. For mud bricks absorb water very easily, whether it comes from the groundwater table or from

rainfall. A mud-brick structure therefore needs to be maintained, repaired, restructured and remodelled. Mud-brick structures are part of a cycle of construction, destruction and repair.

As early as the Neolithic period, but especially in the Bronze Age, mud bricks were used to build houses, villages, towns, and fortifications. In order to compensate for the poor durability of mud bricks, another procedure was introduced in the third millennium BC: terracotta, a process already known from the production of ceramics, gave rise to fired bricks, a material that was lighter and stronger, but at the same time smaller in volume than its predecessor. This meant that more fired bricks had to be produced to build walls. This shortcoming required a continuation in the production of mud bricks and a different use of the two materials: mud bricks were still used for the construction of larger works, such as ramparts, while fired bricks were more often (but not exclusively) used for more modest works in terms of volume, such as houses, monuments, the roofing of mud brick structures, paving and, above all, for aerial structures such as domes, vaults or arches.

The Bronze Age, and especially the Iron Age, saw the birth of empires in the Middle East and Central Asia. The Akkadian Empire, the Sumerian and later the Assyrian, Babylonian or Achaemenid Empires were all built on and through the use of mud and fired bricks.

Even though stone offered greater solidity, for various reasons, mainly related to the supply and mastery of cutting and logistics, the tradition of mud and fired brick remained well anchored in these regions. The arrival of the Greeks in Iran and Central Asia is a perfect illustration of the persistence of brick: new buildings such as Ai-Khanum in Afghanistan show this coexistence of the two materials, in which mud brick was used more than stone.

It was at this time that Bukhara developed as an oasis, inhabited by sedentary rather than nomadic peoples, whose settlement could also be seasonal. There is no evidence of stone construction in this oasis, although the mountains are not so far away. Furthermore, the oasis is geomorphologically located in the delta of the Zerafshan River, which flows from the Alai Mountains in Tajikistan to western Uzbekistan; a situation that makes this area very humid, due to its proximity to the water table and the many water systems. This context made all mud-brick construction very fragile, although this has never stopped the population from building walls, palaces and houses in mud and fired bricks. Mankind has always been able to adapt to the geographical context. In the Bukhara oasis, for example, people found ways of overcoming the situation by building platforms to avoid direct contact between buildings and the ground. Sometimes entire walls were raised from the ground to ensure greater stability of the structures.

During the occupation of the Asiaoi peoples (first-third century AD), Kangju for Chinese sources, the city of Ramitan, today excavated by the archaeological mission of the Louvre Museum, had massive ramparts with square mud-brick towers pierced with loopholes for defence. Later, the royal palace in the centre of the square city was also built in mud brick, revealing architectural skill in the construction of the outer ribs of the walls. In the town of Paykend, on the south-western edge of the oasis, an aristocratic house inhabited by merchants shows a development from the pre-Islamic period to the Islamic period that highlights the mastery of this building material and the way it was modelled in relation to the function and purpose of the building. The Hun populations (late third - mid sixth century), then the Hephthalites, brought with them not only changes in material culture but also the use of fired bricks. These were often trapezoidal in form and were used in the most delicate architectural contexts: arches, vaults, but also the external reinforcement of the defensive walls of buildings such as palaces. In the following period, when the Turkish elite ruled over Sogdia (mid-sixth century – early eighth century), a wall of mud bricks and *pakhsà* (sun-dried mud blocks) was built around a large part of the oasis.

But it was during the Islamic period that a great change took place: the rise of the fired brick. From the tenth century, when Bukhara was the capital of the Samanid dynasty, ruling over a territory stretching from eastern Iran to the Tang border with China, monuments, ramparts, palaces, and houses were built in fired brick. Often mud bricks were used as the inner core for large works such as ramparts, but a fired-brick reinforcement was added for protection, or perhaps also for aesthetic reasons. The Ark (citadel) of Bukhara, which can still be seen today, is built entirely of fired brick, with the sinuous towers that are characteristic of Bukharian fortifications. Since then, fired brick has been the most widely used building material in Bukhara, where mosques, madrasas, hammams, libraries, and simple houses are the result of centuries of expertise and mastery of a material that is easy to find and produce, durable and ecological.

* * * * * *

THE FUTURE OF THE PAST
Thoughts on the Myth of the Labyrinth

Fayçal Tiaïba
Architect and urban planner, founder of the studio Laberinto

"No one thought that the labyrinth and the book were a single object."
Jorge Luis Borges.

A myth that has imposed itself

More than four thousand years ago, a myth as powerful as it is evocative was created on a Mediterranean island. While the Greek historian Herodotus — the first to do so — mentions a labyrinth in Egypt in the fifth century BC, describing it as a memorial to themselves by the kings of each of the twelve regions of Egypt,[1] it is without a doubt the Greek myth of the labyrinth of Crete that has imposed itself everywhere, through time and space.

This apparently simple story conceals a depth and subtlety that is very out of the ordinary. It resonates today with a disturbing modernity that is worthy of our consideration here. This is the story in a nutshell: Minos, king of Crete, commissions Daedalus, his architect, to design a structure to imprison the Minotaur, a monstrous creature that is half man, half bull, born of his wife Pasiphae's bout of passion with a white bull.[2]

Daedalus did not imagine a building, but a series of corridors and dead ends from which it would be impossible to escape once inside: this was the labyrinth. In his *Metamorphoses*, Ovid describes it as "a habitation of many divisions, and an abode full of mazes. Daedalus, a man highly celebrated for his skill in architecture, planned the work, and confounded the marks of distinction, and led the eyes into mazy wanderings, by the intricacy of its various passages." The Minotaur was forced into the centre of the labyrinth and abandoned to his fate, unable to escape.

It was here that he was eventually killed by Theseus, son of the king of Athens, who had come to Crete to put an end to the sacrifice of young Athenians to the Minotaur by King Minos. He escaped with the help of Ariadne, Minos' daughter, who fell in love with him and gave him the solution Daedalus had devised to escape the labyrinth: a ball of wool that Theseus was to unroll as he moved through the labyrinth. This, of course, was Ariadne's thread. His feat accomplished, Theseus escaped by following the thread and left the island with Ariadne, infuriating Minos.

As a result, Minos imprisoned Daedalus and his son Icarus in the labyrinth. But the ingenious architect made a pair of wings for himself and his son by arranging feathers in a row and tying them together with linen in the middle and wax at the bottom. Before launching into the air, Daedalus warned young Icarus not to fly too low, as he risked damaging the wings in the sea, or not too high, as the sun would melt the wax and destroy them. But, giving in to the sun's lure, Icarus flew higher and higher, and his wings disintegrated. He fell into the sea that now bears his name.

Symbols of the labyrinth

This is the story of the labyrinth of Daedalus, in which Asterion the Minotaur was trapped. The ancient myths have a primary, universal, and timeless force, rooted in the depths of the human soul. And this one is no exception. That is why it has given rise to so many interpretations and metaphors. For many, it is the myth of myths, whose symbol, a graffiti of childlike simplicity, has been found on pottery, coins, temple columns, cathedral mosaics, and in gardens. Minoan labyrinth coins have been found in Pompeii, on the island of Sumatra and as far away as Rio Paraguay.

Paolo Santarcangeli writes in his book *Le livre des labyrinthes*: "To speak of the labyrinth with a complete knowledge of all the aspects it can adopt, one would have to be an ethnologist, an archaeologist, a specialist in the history of religions and of prehistory, [...] an architect, a gardener and many other things; but above all one would have to be a poet."[3] Artists and thinkers have all made use of the myth. It runs through Dante Alighieri's *Divine Comedy*,[4] through the work of Picasso and the literature of Jorge Luis Borges,[5] a writer obsessed with it.

To speak of the labyrinth is to prepare oneself for an encounter with oneself and with the world. This myth mixes fear and hope. Our fear of the future and its uncertainty, for tomorrow is as unknown to us as the next meander in the labyrinth. And every step we take is like a new day. The Minotaur, and with him death, may be lurking there. Even if there is still hope lurking deep within us. This story is such that it both attracts and repels us, reminding us of our human and animal nature. But what other meaning can this myth have?

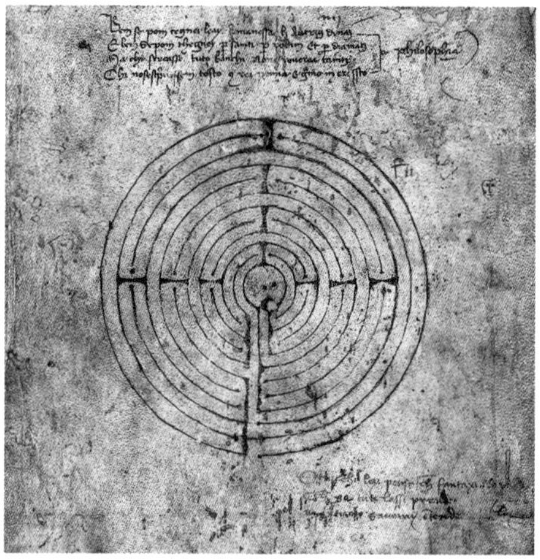

From the labyrinth to network science

The labyrinth symbolises the bubbling of our minds, because this myth also speaks of a way of thinking that would change the world. "The human mind is more capable of thinking of labyrinths than its opposite," says Umberto Eco.[6] Our way of thinking is as complex as a labyrinth offset by the solution, Ariadne's thread, the latter undoing the former. "This Ariadne's thread is presented in the legend as the way out of the labyrinth, when in fact it was actually the labyrinth itself."[7] The essential question is: how do we navigate the labyrinth? Or how do we extract a linear thought from the intuitive chaos of our mind? This is the very definition of an algorithm, understood as a finite and unambiguous sequence of instructions and operations making it possible to resolve a class of problems. An algorithm whose etymology derives from Al-Khawarizmi, a mathematician born in Khiva, in what is now Uzbekistan. Ariadne's thread thus represents a ball of thread that has become a homing device or search engine. This ancient discovery is the basis of network science. Pierre Rosenstiehl, a mathematician with a passion for labyrinths, sums it up as follows: "The Minoans sensed that the world is complex to describe, like a labyrinth, while the thought that theorises it is, like an Ariadne's thread, a succession of evidences."[8] And here we are, propelled from antiquity to modernity and its new technologies. In a virtual world, a networked world.

The network, which is one of the three forms of the labyrinth.[9] And like the labyrinth, it always has a heart at the centre, which we call the processor, but also the core. All the paths that data take lead to it. And while we often have the feeling of being lost when we think of networks (and especially the largest of them, the Internet), the possibility of resolution always lies at its core.

In the myth of Theseus and the Minotaur, the centre crystallises the turning point of the story, the place where a violent death occurs, but where the resolution of the conflict also takes place, bringing peace and comfort to a greater number, sometimes at the price of sacrifice. On leaving the labyrinth, Theseus is reborn and order is restored. Thus, one does not always get lost in the labyrinth. One can also find oneself in it, so long as one goes through it and faces one's personal contradictions and fears.

Far from the traumatising images and meanings with which the myth is too often associated, the labyrinth represents above all an initiatory journey, the passing of a test, a resurrection. It symbolises courage, but also human genius in the person of Daedalus, who goes from find to find, overcoming all the challenges that are placed before him.

Perfection seen from above

What this myth illustrates is the very essence of the profession of architecture. It tells of the encounter between a client (Minos) who has identified a precise need — in this case, to imprison the Minotaur — and who calls upon a creator (Daedalus) to design an architectural solution (the labyrinth). It can be seen as the first commission for an architect.

But while the perfection of the labyrinth lies in the complexity of its plan, its *raison d'être* lies in the absolute secrecy that must surround its design. Seen from above, its ingenuity is inoperative, for there is then no way to ensure anyone loses himself. That is why it had to be forbidden to see the labyrinth from above. Daedalus and his son saw it briefly as they flew over it. Daedalus knew his plan, having conceived it. Icarus, on the other hand, saw beneath his eyes the forks, the paths, the dead ends, the beauty of the work. Perhaps it was the violation of this mystery that condemned him, not the sun.

Building at human height

Isn't all architecture only relevant when seen, felt and experienced from the ground? Shouldn't the architect only design at human height? Designing from the ground up and *from* the ground itself. It is said that a handful of earth contains more organised information than the surface of all the known planets put together. Why not just bend down and pick it up? Transform it, shape it, bake it, mark it.

There is an earthen citadel in Khwarizm, Uzbekistan. This ruin, which looks strangely like a labyrinth, is called Toprak-Qala. A brick lies on the ground, detached from the walls of the monumental structure. It has been dragged, moved. It is broken on both sides, but what remains of it suggests it was a very large brick. It is a piece of earth that has stood the test of time and continues to do so.

Despite the passage of centuries and the increasing frequency of tourist visits. Its presence is unusual, almost miraculous.

We observe it, we photograph it. A mysterious detail stands out: two deep lines mark one of its faces. They are drawn by hand. With a finger, to be precise. This mark is a sort of signature made by one of the stonemasons who built this citadel.[10] Almost two thousand years ago.

Each brick contains all the material of which history is made.

"You put together two people who have not been put together before; and sometimes the world is changed, sometimes not. They may crash and burn, or burn and crash. But sometimes, something new is made, and then the world is changed," writes Julian Barnes in his book *Levels of Life*, unconsciously evoking Icarus. You bring Theseus and Ariadne together and love is born. You bring Theseus and the Minotaur together and a myth is created.

* * * * * *

NOTES

[1] *Herodotus goes even further by stating that "the labyrinth also wins the comparison with the pyramids."*

[2] *Minos vowed to sacrifice to Poseidon the marvellous animal that the God of the Seas had offered him, but he sacrificed another bull instead. Enraged, Poseidon took his revenge and made Pasiphae, the ruler's wife, fall madly in love with the White Bull.*

[3] *Paolo Santarcangeli,* Le livre des labyrinthes, *Paris: Gallimard, 1974.*

[4] *The circles of the underworld are directly inspired by a circular labyrinth. Almost all the protagonists are mentioned in several places: Minos, Pasiphae, the Minotaur, Theseus, and Icarus.*

[5] *Read among others the short stories "The Two Kings and the Two Labyrinths", "Ibn Hakkan Al-Bokhari, Murdered in his Labyrinth" or "The Garden of Forking Paths."*

[6] *Umberto Eco, in his preface to the collective work* Labyrinths *by Franco Maria Ricci, New York: Rizzoli, 2013.*

[7] *Umberto Eco,* From the Tree to the Labyrinth, *Cambridge, MA: Harvard University Press, 2014.*

[8] *Pierre Rosenstiehl,* Le labyrinthe des jours ordinaires, *Paris : Editions du Seuil, 2013.*

[9] *According to Umberto Eco, the three types of labyrinths are the unicursal, the maze and the net. From* Le livre des labyrinthes, *cit., 1974.*

[10] *The archaeologists Claude Rapin and Guy Lecuyot have drawn from this type of marks an admirable study and synthesis, with supporting drawings and figures. Read "Samarkand and Aï Khanoum, marked bricks in Central Asia," in* Actes du colloque international: La brique antique et médiévale, production et commercialisation d'un matériau, *Saint-Cloud, 16–18 November 1995.*

INTUITIONS

Studio KO, Karl Fournier and Olivier Marty
Architects, founders of Studio KO

© Noël Manalili.

The only thing that can balance the weight of reality is the power of imagination.
Necessary intention.
Freedom that can be vertiginous but that is nevertheless the driving force behind creation. It requires maintaining a safe distance from theories, knowing them in order to better circumvent them, understanding them without becoming their slave. It also means being wary of trends and the pleasant fragrance of the zeitgeist, which anaesthetizes critical thinking through the lightning speed of its propagation. It implies abandoning any attempt at style, which is simply a way of bringing the focus back onto oneself. It is about leaving the shores of certainty and flirting with doubt, in order to better embrace one's sensitive context.

Why context?
It would be so much simpler to ignore it, but we must refuse the easy way out. Because context is about what has happened in the past, and what remains of it. For what context teaches us when we are prepared to look, listen, and scrutinize it. For its complex ramifications that nourish a project. Archaeology, geology, poetry of the landscape. For what it says about man and the struggle that has played out between nature and mankind, who takes whatever nature has to offer that is essential for survival. It is about domestication, traces, and respect.

Because we have faith in rural common sense, in the everyday necessities that forged built landscapes before the industrial revolutions. Not out of an excessive taste for the past, but because there is so much to learn from the way in which several houses fit together to protect themselves from a prevailing wind, in how shade was created and sunlight allowed to enter. In the way each material was used for what it had to offer in its raw state: its resistance to rain, its density, its capacity to bridge a void, or to be compressed.

A time in which scale and spatial proportion were but precise expressions of man's needs. A frugality that questions the monumentality of modern-day constructions.

The underlying notion of a perfect and just balance, which can only be achieved by understanding the context, is fundamental. Because architecture is always intended to fill a need, it should be as balanced and apt as possible. Justness is an indispensable prerequisite to the emergence of beauty, which, needless to say, is not a dirty word. Beauty has the unique ability to reach out across eras, far beyond the simple moment of its creation. Beauty alone escapes the grip of time, and can turn back to gaze at it. Not beauty for beauty's sake, but for its enduring force of resistance to the uniformity of the world.

Look at the countrysides of Europe, the planted terraces of the Atlas Mountains, the steppes of Karakalpakstan: at all the small things, so often insignificant yet beautiful, that possess the power of the obvious, of the harsh conditions that prompted their invention. It is by their abstraction, their simplicity, and their ability to withstand the test of time that they are relevant today. And it is this relevance that we call modernity.

Make no mistake, this is not about nostalgia, pastiche, or folklore.

We have no other intention than to belong to our time; if we are infatuated with modernity, it is of a rooted modernity. Archaic.

* * * * * *

ANNOTATED ILLUSTRATIONS

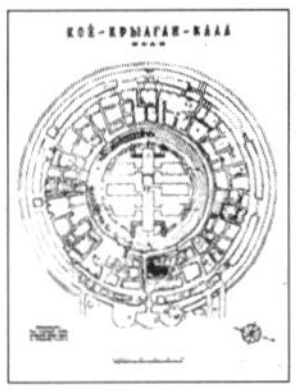

Cover
Koi Krylgan-Qala, survey drawing

S. P. Tolstov, *Ancient Khorezm*, Moscow: MSU, 1948

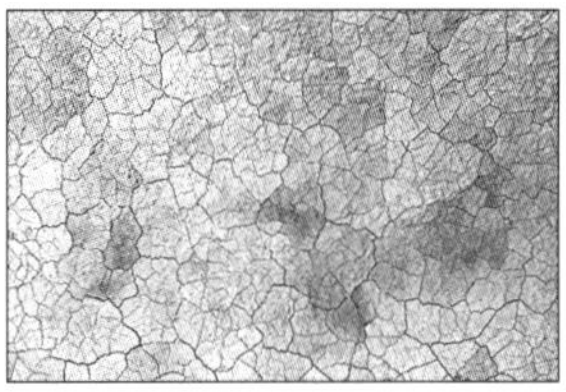

Endpaper
Toprak-Qala, Karakalpakstan Uzbekistan, 2023

© Sophia Bengebara

Page 1
Linear B Tablet (PY Cn 1287), end of the thirteenth century BC, Pylos (Peloponnese, Greece)

Mycenean palace of Ano Eglianos (known as "the Palace of Nestor"), National Archaeological Museum, Athens, NAM Π 24120
© Hellenic Ministry of Culture and Sports/Organization for the Management and Development of Cultural Resources

Page 2
Koy Krylgan-Qala, Karakalpakstan Uzbekistan, 2023

© Kamila Rustembekova

Page 4
Hotel Uzbekistan, Tashkent Uzbekistan, 2023

© Emine Gözde Sevim

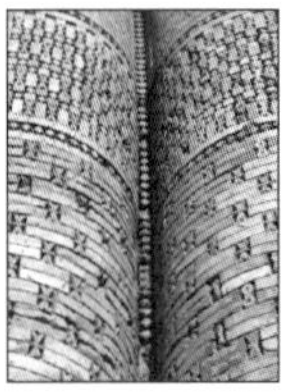

Page 7
Mausoleum of Abu Ibrahim Ismail, Bukhara Uzbekistan, 2023

© El Mehdi Azzam

Page 8
Alisher Navoi/Panorama Cinema, Tashkent Uzbekistan, 2023

© Emine Gözde Sevim

Page 10
Chorsu Bazaar, Tashkent, Uzbekistan, 2023

© Emine Gözde Sevim

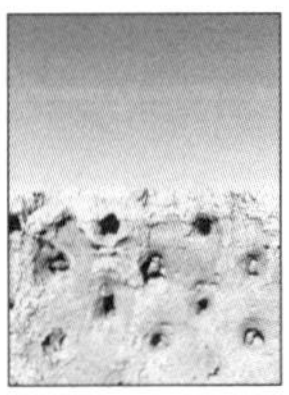

Page 11
Toprak-Qala, Karakalpakstan, Uzbekistan, 2023

© Fayçal Tiaïba

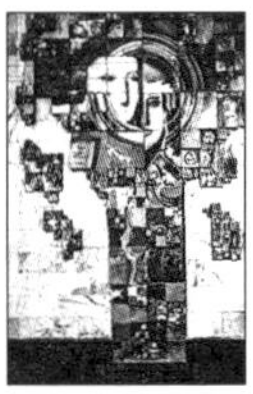

Page 12
Gafur Gulom Metro station, Tashkent, Uzbekistan, 2023

© Emine Gözde Sevim

Page 13
Fragment of a Mural Painting Depicting a Human Face, Toprak-Qala, second–third century

23.5 × 20 cm, The State Hermitage Museum, St. Petersburg, Inv. no. XP-833
Photograph © The State Hermitage Museum/photo by Inna Regentova

Page 14
Gafur Gulom Metro station, Tashkent, Uzbekistan, 2023

© Emine Gözde Sevim

Page 15
Detail of a mosque, Bukhara, Uzbekistan, 2023

© Kamila Rustembekova

Page 16
Ayaz-Qala, Karakalpakstan, Uzbekistan, 2023

© Emine Gözde Sevim

Page 18
Museum of Arts of Uzbekistan, Tashkent, 2023

© Karl Fournier

Page 19
Toprak-Qala, Karakalpakstan, Uzbekistan, 2023

© Karl Fournier

Page 20
Ayaz-Qala, Karakalpakstan, Uzbekistan, 2023

© Emine Gözde Sevim

Page 22
Etienne Jules Ramey (1796–1852), Theseus and the Minotaur, 1821

Tuileries Garden, Paris
© Javier Palmieri/Alamy Stock Photo

Page 23
Stater from Knossos, Labyrinth, 300–270 BC

Greek coin, reverse side, silver, Crete, Knossos, Henry Seyrig Fund, Bibliothèque nationale de France, ACQ 1973-1-115
Bibliothèque National de France

Page 45
V. Savitsky, Sunset over Koy Kirilgan-Qala

Oil on canvas, 44.5 × 26 cm
The State Museum of Arts of the Republic of Karakalpakstan

Page 47
Andrey Arakelyan, Ramparts of the citadel of Bukhara

The Art and Culture Development Foundation (ACDF), the Cabinet of Ministers of the Republic of Uzbekistan

Page 50
Master of the Campana Cassoni, Theseus and the Minotaur, between 1510 and 1520

Poplar (wood), oil on panel, 69 × 155 cm
Campana Collection, Musée du Petit Palais, Avignon, Inv. no. MI528
© Musee du Petit Palais, Avignone, Francia/Rmn Grand Palais/René-Gabriel Ojéda/Dist. Foto SCALA, Firenze, 2023

Page 51
Asterion, The Minotaur, sculpture

Roman copy of the 5th century c. before our era. Sculptural group erected in the Acropolis. Found in Plaka, Athens.
Preserved height of the statue: 73 cm
National Archaeological Museum, Athens
© DeAgostini Picture Library/Scala, Firenze, 2023

Page 52
Dante Alighieri (1265–1321), The Divine Comedy (Divina Commedia)

Folio 175, Labyrinth, medieval, Bibliothèque nationale de France, MS8530
Bibliothèque National de France

Page 53
Auguste Gaspard Louis Boucher-Desnoyers (1779–1857), Daedalus and Icarus

1800, print, Bibliothèque nationale de France, Reserve AA-5
Bibliothèque National de France

Page 55
Paul Nadar, Horse market at the foot of the mosque in Samarkand. Paul Nadar's voyage to Russian Turkestan in 1890

Gelatin silver bromide glass negative, 3 × 4 cm, Médiathèque de l'Architecture et du Patrimoine, Charenton-le-Pont, Inv. no. NDR06348B
Patrimoine, Charenton-le-Pont, Francia/Rmn Grand Palais/Paul Nadar/Dist. Foto SCALA, Firenze, 2023

CONTRIBUTORS

El Mehdi Azzam. *After studying engineering and physical sciences, El Mehdi Azzam developed an interest in cinema, which he studied in Morocco and then in France. The films he has directed have won awards at several festivals (Grand Prix in San Sebastian, Young Audience Prize at Cinémed, SACD Prize, Canal+ Prize, and others). He has collaborated with Studio KO on three creative films (*Almost KO, 'E', Tentative désespérée pour définir la patrie*). He is currently doing a PhD at the Université Jean Jaurès in Toulouse, on the aesthetic impact of Artificial Intelligence on the cinematographic language.*

Miza Mucciarelli. *Born in Brescia, Northern Italy, in 1976. Miza moved to Paris for studies following her degree in Architecture at the Milan Polytechnic. After graduation, she started directing the Model Lab at Dominique Perrault Architecture. In January 2009 she founded her own independent lab, Ateliermisto, specialising in high-end models that fuse the unique craftsmanship skills of her region with precious materials such as marble and other stones, special woods, and metals. She is constantly experimenting and discovering new approaches to play with. As a result, Miza's models are conceived as sculptural works of art yearning to translate the essence of the spaces represented and the sensory experiences associated with them.*

Emine Gözde Sevim *(Istanbul, 1985) is an artist acclaimed for her narratives of lives amidst historic changes. Her work focuses on the experiences of individuals at times when news stories grab the headlines, in an attempt to create "alternative" visual narratives of history. She graduated from Bard College (USA) in 2008. Her work has been exhibited, published and recognized by awards and grants internationally. She is the author of* Embed in Egypt *(Kehrer Verlag, 2015) and is the first and so far only Turkish-born recipient of the coveted Magnum Foundation Fund. She lives in Brooklyn, New York.*

Irina Arzhantseva *graduated from the Department of Archaeology, Moscow State University (MGU). She holds a PhD in History, specialising in Central Asian archaeology and interdisciplinary methods of archaeological research. She is currently Principal Researcher in the Institute of Ethnology and Anthropology, Russian Academy of Sciences. She has led several expeditions in the North Caucasus, Tuva, and Kazakhstan, and is currently leading an archaeological excavation at the Dzhankent site. As a historian of science, her main interest is the history of the Khorezmian Archaeological Ethnographic Expedition. She is the author of four books and over 150 scholarly papers.*

Oktyabr Dospanov *(Nukus, 1962) is an archaeologist and PhD in History. He currently heads the archaeological department at the Savitsky State Art Museum and specialises in studying myths and reflections of catastrophes in folklore, as well as archaeological evidence from the past. He worked his way up from conservator of ceramics to the head of the archaeological department. He has participated in and led numerous international expeditions in the region. Dospanov is the author of several scientific publications on cultural heritage, archaeology, ecology, ethnography, and the development of the tourism potential of the Republic of Karakalpakstan.*

Rocco Rante *is an archaeologist at the Louvre Museum and qualified at the University La Sorbonne-Panthéon.*
He directs the archaeological mission in Khorasan and the archaeological mission in the oasis of Bukhara.
He recently published two volumes of the trilogy The Oasis of Bukhara *in the Brill series, 2019 and 2022, the second one in collaboration with Florian Schwarz and Luigi Tronca.*
He previously edited Greater Khorasan, *De Gruyter, 2015, and* Rayy: from its Origins to the Mongol Invasion, *Brill, 2015.*
He recently edited the exhibition catalogue The Splendours of Uzbekistan's Oases.

Fayçal Tiaïba *(Chambéry, France, 1974) is an architect and urban planner. He graduated from the Polytechnical School of Architecture in Algiers in 1997 and did his postgraduate studies at La Sorbonne University in Paris, specializing in historical heritage and urban mutations.*
After studying architecture, he obtained a degree in computer science followed by a career in the field of algorithms and database development.
After working with Shigeru Ban in Paris, he joined Studio KO in 2011 in Marrakech for the Yves Saint Laurent Museum project (2017). He later became a partner. He is the founder of Laberinto, a multidisciplinary studio based in Marrakech and Paris.

Uzbekistan
Art and Culture
Development
Foundation

Uzbekistan
National
Pavilion

The Uzbekistan Art and Culture Development Foundation under the Cabinet of Ministers of the Republic of Uzbekistan, founded in 2017 by the decree of President Shavkat Mirziyoyev, fosters international cooperation and promotes the culture of Uzbekistan on the international stage.
It showcases national heritage by initiating projects in the fine arts, architecture, literature, theater, music, craft, design and dance.
The mission of the Foundation is to create an inclusive and accessible environment in the country's cultural institutions, to contribute to the renovation of museums, and to develop cultural patronage and professional training for the arts and culture sector.

TABLE OF CONTENTS

UNBUILD TOGETHER

Archaism vs Modernity

WORKSHOPS: A PERSONAL DIARY BY EMINE GÖZDE SEVIM

Two workshops, organised with the support of the Foundation for Art and Culture of the Republic of Uzbekistan, involved 25 architecture students from Ajou University in Tashkent (AUT). They took place from the 9th to the 21st of January 2023 in three different locations: Tashkent, Bukhara, and Karakalpakstan, sometimes in extremely cold conditions.

For the Uzbek pavilion at the Venice Architecture Biennale, following the example of the "laboratory" described by Lesley Lokko, it came to us naturally to create a collective work centered on a sensitive architectural installation that the public would be invited to walk through, touch, and feel.

This intuition took shape through two workshops that we held with 25 architecture students from the AUT of Tashkent, and three associated artists. Since we are neither professors nor theorists, but simply practitioners, we wanted to share with the students certain themes related to the problems of our time as well as others dear to our own architectural practice: materiality, context, archaism, modernity.

This joint work was carried out in two ways:

First, by theoretical research starting with visits to three Qalas: the Zoroastrian ruins of Karakalpakstan. By thus feeding our imagination, we prepared ourselves to face the scenographic challenges of the Biennale Pavilion. There, the idea of a labyrinthian form was discussed. Throughout this journey, we invited the students to question the notions of modernity and context.

Second, by practical research through experimentation with material, from earth to brick, which led us to Bukhara to the master ceramist Abdulvahid Bukhoriy. With him we learned the techniques of hot glazing, and tried to push its limits. We realized that this historical material emanating from the earth had nearly disappeared from construction methods. It seemed relevant to us to integrate it into our research in order to make the students aware of a savoir-faire whose survival is threatened. To see the relevance of reintroducing this material, which responds to many current constraints. The fact that we don't need to look for this modernity elsewhere, globally, but that it is already present here, locally.

We also did research employing the notion of scale, as we discovered together the architectural form of the 1:1 wood mock-up and subsequently adapted it with the precious help of the plastic artist and model maker Miza Mucciarelli.

This invitation to travel within a country and its history, along with the questioning of the traces that were left to us, nourished the material necessary for the project. The traces patiently collected during the sessions, relics of the students' work, discussions, and exchanges which through El Mehdi Azzam's film projected at the core of the installation and Emine Gözde Sevim's photographic diary freeze this moment in time. A unique moment that leaves room for contemplation, for an awareness of things.

The aim of these workshops was to arouse the students' curiosity as well as to teach them how to respond to a given problem. To help them rediscover their own culture from an exterior viewpoint, a viewpoint that invites them to see certain small or underestimated things.

It has been an adventure above all human, another way of practicing our art, to which the following pages bear witness.

Studio KO

TOSHKENT

WORKSHOP 1, January 2023
Archaism vs modernity

Day 1 - 9th January
Ajou University in Tashkent
> Introduction of the workshop team: Studio KO, AUT professors and students, associated artists
> Introduction to the Biennale's theme, workshop objectives, and schedule
> Introduction of the two "reporter" students that would participate in both workshops
> Presentation of Studio KO's approach to architectural practice
> Introduction of the four research themes: Context, Pivotal moments in history, Ruins, and Labyrinths.

Day 2 - 10th January
State Museum of Arts of Uzbekistan, Tashkent
> Discussion of preliminary research
> Group work on the themes
> Presentation of the finalised theme research and discussion about workshop methods
> Lecture on Ancient Khorezm archaeological expeditions by Irina Arzhantseva.

Day 3 - 11th January
State Museum of Arts of Uzbekistan, Tashkent
> Presentation of the Venice pavilion project: context and constraints
> Group work on the installation project: scenography layout and other installation proposals.

Day 4 - 12th January
Qalas sites, Karakalpakstan
> Travel to Urgench by plane then to Qalas sites by car
> Visit of Toprak Qala site: discovery and discussion
> Travel to hotel in Urgench.

Day 5 - 13th January
Qalas sites, Karakalpakstan
> Visit of Koi Krylgan Qala site: discovery and discussion
> Travel back to Tashkent.

Day 6 - 14th January
State Museum of Arts of Uzbekistan, Tashkent
> Finalizing student research in small groups
> Presentation of students' research and project proposals
> Presentation of Studio KO proposal for the Venice pavilion: discussion
> Presentation of Emine Gözde Sevim work
> Conclusion.

WORKSHOP 2, January 2023
Brick, from clay to wall

Day 1 - 17th January
Ajou University in Tashkent
> Introduction of the workshop team: Studio KO, AUT professors and students, associated artists
> Introduction to the Biennale theme, workshop objectives and schedule
> Presentation of Studio KO's approach to architectural practice
> Presentation of Miza Mucciarelli: model work and and materiality research
> Report on first workshop by the two "reporter" students.

Day 2 - 18th January
Abdulvahid Bukhoriy's atelier, Bukhara
> Morning: travel to Bukhara by train then to hotel
> Feedback during the train trip on preliminary research
> Old Bukhara visit: Mausoleum of the Samanids Tap-i-Tilpak Furushon Magoki Attari Mosque, understanding cladding and ornamentation
> Presentation of Abdulvahid and his work: enamel glazing process
> Exercise 1: realisation of enamel glazing prototypes on handmade bricks.

Day 3 - 19th January
Abdulvahid Bukhoriy's atelier, Bukhara
> Exercise 2: conception of a brick wall prototype: size of module, patterns, perception
> Follow-up of exercise 1 at Abdulvahid's atelier: discovery of the glazing result after baking.

Day 4 - 20th January
CCA Diesel Station, Tashkent
> Morning: travel back to Tashkent by plane
> Discovery of the mock up by the students at the Diesel station: experience, necessary adjustments (height, thickness, etc.)
> Follow-up of exercise 2: scale modelling of the walls with Miza Mucciarelli
> Discussion and definition of the drawings to be produced for the students' final presentations: plans, sections, elevations, 3D renderings.

Day 5 - 21st January
CCA Diesel Station, Tashkent
> Exercise 3: students' realisation of a wall prototype: bonds, patterns, details
> Students' final presentation: prototypes and drawings
> Conclusion (with all the students from both workshops).

Plan
Dimensions

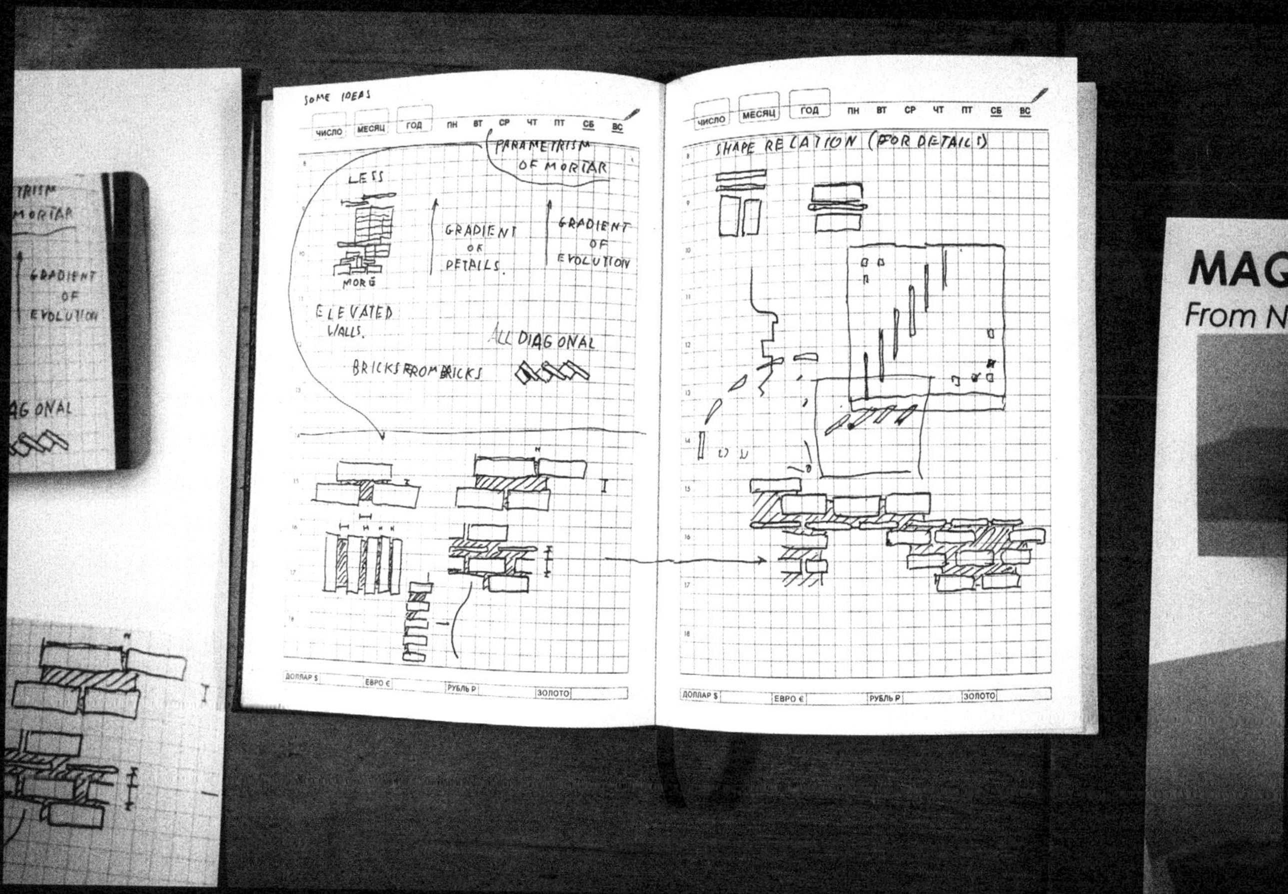
SOME IDEAS
ЧИСЛО МЕСЯЦ ГОД ПН ВТ СР ЧТ ПТ СБ ВС
PARAMETRISM OF MORTAR
LESS
MORE
GRADIENT OF DETAILS
GRADIENT OF EVOLUTION
ELEVATED WALLS
ALL DIAGONAL
BRICKS FROM BRICKS
SHAPE RELATION (FOR DETAILS)
ДОЛЛАР $ ЕВРО € РУБЛЬ Р ЗОЛОТО
MAQ
From N

LOUVIERS

WORKSHOPS PARTICIPANTS

Studio KO

Karl Fournier	Partner Architect
Olivier Marty	Partner Architect
Jean-Baptiste Carisé	Architect
Sophia Bengebara	Architect

Ajou University in Tashkent

Management

Oh Seokkyu	Dean of the Architecture Department
Farkhod Rikhsiev	Professor

Students

Madina Atajonova, Abrorjon Abdusattorov, Viktoriya Anshakova, Aziza Askarova, Miraziz Baymatov, Melissa Danaeva, Jakhongir Eshnazarov, Ramziddin Gayratov, Khayitali Gofurov, Farangis Gopilova, Samandar Ibrokhimov, Salge Islyamova, Ulugbek Jumambetov, Shirina Karieva, Jasmina Khalmatova, Yusufjon Komiljonov, Munisa Khudaybergenova, Dinara Mirzoraimova, Nizomiddin Narzullaev, Oydinoy Ochilboeva, Ravshankhon Kodirov, Raufkhon Shavkatkhonov, Afruzkhon Yakhyoev, Azizbek Yulchiev, Sunnatulla Zayniddinov

Associated Artists

El Mehdi Azzam	Filmmaker
Abdulvahid Bukhoriy	Master ceramist
Miza Mucciarelli	Architect, sculptor & model maker
Emine Gözde Sevim	Photographer

Participants

Fayçal Tiaïba	Catalogue Curator
Irina Arzhantseva	Archeologist
Kamila Rustembekova	Photographer

CREDITS

Special Support
Saïda Mirziyoyeva, Head of the Communications and Information Policy Section of the Administration of the President of the Republic of Uzbekistan

Commissioner
Gayane Umerova, Executive Director of the Art and Culture Development Foundation under the Cabinet of Ministers of the Republic of Uzbekistan

Curators
Studio KO.
Karl Fournier & Olivier Marty,
Jean-Baptiste Carisé, Sophia Bengebara

Artists
El Mehdi Azzam, Miza Mucciarelli,
Emine Gözde Sevim, Abdulvokhid Bukhoriy

Head of Project
Madina Badalova, Uzbekistan Art and Culture Development Foundation

Project Managers
Boburkhon Mamatkhodjaev, Irina Yan, Laziza Akbarova, Uzbekistan Art and Culture Development Foundation

Head of Communications and Public Policy
Anastasia Sinitsyna, Uzbekistan Art and Culture Development Foundation

Communication and PR
Claudine Colin Communications, Karla Otto

Curator of the Catalogue
Fayçal Tiaïba / Laberinto

Graphic Identity, Editing and Digital Content
Izhak, Nathalie Franck, Laure Frey
and Louis Brunet

Exhibition Design
Studio KO

Exhibition Installation
We Exhibit
Davide De Carlo, production coordinator
Elena Bongiorno, production manager
Alessandra Dal Mos, installation supervision

Repro and printing
Opero s.r.l., Verona

First edition May 2023.
for Marsilio Editori® s.p.a., Venezia

Available through ARTBOOK | D.A.P. 75 Broad Street Suite 630 New York NY 10004 www.artbook.com